SIMPLY

POETIC

SOPHIA ASMAH'S BOOKS

MATHS FICTION SERIES:

MY BIRTHDAY IS ON SATURDAY
BY SOPHIA ASMAH

SUMMER IN NUMBERVILLE
BY SOPHIA ASMAH

SIMPLY POETIC

SOPHIA ASMAH

SOPHIA ASMAH PUBLISHERS

Accra, Ghana

Published by Sophia Asmah Publishers
Email: sophiaasmahbooks@gmail.com
Facebook: Sophia Asmah Books
Twitter: @SophiAsmahBooks
Instagram: @SophiaAsmahBooks

To Isabel
my daughter

ACKNOWLEDGEMENTS

Thanks to God for providing all my daily needs and for keeping me in this 'writing space.'

This poetry book is all because of you, Isabel. You told me to 'write something else' and I listened to you. Now, here I am with my collection of poems.

Also, thanks Isabel for all the times you shared your opinion, when I interrupted you for it.

Lynn, there is no limitation on the number of times I am allowed to say thank you, so get ready to live with it.

To the one person in the world, who I feel comfortable enough with; to say I am stuck... you are my angel on earth.

J.B., who would have thought you, could be more excited about my books than I am. You are truly one in a million.

Emma, where should I start? You still remain my very good friend after all these years. Thanks for being you.

Class of 1983, you are not just my classmates but you are also my friends. Thank you. I will also like to say thank you to Gloria, Julie, Wilhemina, Kudirat and Barbara. It's the little things which matter most.

Felix, I gave you my first manuscript to read and you only had positive comments Thank you for the morale booster.

I would also like to say that, I am immensely grateful to my parents for everything.

Finally, thanks to everyone for reading what I write... I am still writing.

CONTENTS

PART 1 CURRENT LOCATION   1
            PLANET EARTH

WILL YOU DO IT?   3
PER-FEC-TION5   5
BREATHE   9
ONE OF THOSE DAYS   15
YOU SHOULD21   21
TOTAL BEAUTY   27
DON'T JUST   31

PART 2   THAT FEELING   35
LOVE IS IN THE AIR   37
MAKE THAT CALL   41

YOU STILL LOVE ME   47

WINDOWS OF MY HEART   51

LOVE   57

DON'T LOOK BACK   61

PART 3   POLY-TICS   65

I AM A CONTINENT   67

MY COLOURS   71

DISCOMBOBULATING DILEMMA   79

SPEAK UP   83

DON'T TAKE AWAY MY FREEDOM   89

SAY IT AS IT IS   93

PRESS ON. INCH FORWARD!   101

PART 4   FORGET THE 'TO DO'   107

SOUL FOOD RESTAURANT   109

ON THAT WARM BRIDGE   117

TANGO AMONGST THE CLOUDS   127

PART 5   MATHE-MATI-CALLY   137
POETIC

ONE PLUS ONE   139

GEO-ME-TREE   143

PIE NOT PI (π)   147

OVER ONE   153

PART 6   MYSTIC   157

PLEASE DON'T STAND STILL   159

MAGIC   167

THANK YOU   171

APPENDIX: ADINKRA SYMBOLS   175

PART 1

CURRENT LOCATION: PLANET EARTH

2

WILL YOU DO IT ?

You said you will do it...
Could you have done it?
Did you try to do it?
Why didn't you do it?

I said I would do it...
I knew I could do it!
I tried to do it!
Okay, I will make sure...
I finish it!

4

PER-FEC-TION

Nothing is ever perfect
I used to think it was.

And can you say...
I could be blamed...
For thinking that
There's nothing like
Per-fec-tion

From the happily ever after
To the lights are on each day
I would never have dreamt...
That this world I live in
Could be any less than...
What we choose to call
Per-fec-tion.

Alas!
Lo and behold!
There is no happily ever after
The bright lights...
Do go off...
From time to time.

So can I now, go back...
And live those years, again
So that...
I will grow up knowing...
There's nothing in life
Like Per-fec-tion.

BREATHE

When the phone rings
And it's all bad news

Your heart is...
ThUMPiNg

Your head is ...
PuMpInG.

Just take a moment
And remember to...
B

R

E

A

T

H

E.

10

When you turn on the TV
And you hear the words,
'It is tragic...'
Your heart is **ThUmPiNg**
Your head is **PuMpInG.**

Just take a moment
And remember to...
B
  R
   E
    A
     T
      H
       E.

When you sit your exams
And the results are in
Your heart is **ThUmPiNg**
Your head is **PuMpInG.**

Just take a moment
And remember to...
B
 R
  E
   A
    T
     H
      E.

12

B
R
E
A
T
H
E...

And keep on...

B
R
E
A
T
H
I
N
G!

13

14

ONE OF THOSE DAYS

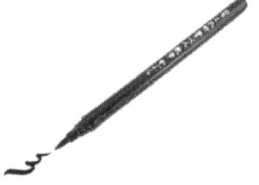

Early in the morning
I arise.

It's so silent
I can hear a pin drop.

Where are the birds?
I do not hear them sing.

15

I look out the window
I cannot see a thing...

Chirp, chirp, chirp
I think I hear them now.

And I wonder...
What will this day bring?

Late at night
I lie down to sleep.

This time the silence evades
The deep, dark night.

16

I hear the crickets, once again
Could that be
Some croaking too?

I start to replay
The day's events.

Suddenly...
There's only silence.

It's now time
To close my eyes
And get that sleep
I so deserve.

This has most definitely been...
One of those days
I'm sure, I will never forget.

19

20

YOU SHOULD

IF you can
You should.

If you can not
You should...

I SHOULD?

Wait a minute...
You should...
At least try!

21

If you can dance
You should.

If you can not dance
You should...

I SHOULD?

Wait a minute...
You should...
At least try!

IF you can sing
You should.

If you can not sing
You should...

I SHOULD?

Wait a minute...
You should...
At least try!

IF you can write
You should.

If you can not write
You should...

23

I SHOULD?

Wait a minute...
You should...
At least try!

IF you can dream
You should.

If you can not dream
You should...

I SHOULD?

24

Wait a minute...
You should...
At least
Give it a try...
And do your best!

26

TOTAL BEAUTY

BEAUTY on the outside
No BEAUTY on the inside
Could that define
The true sense of
TOTAL BEAUTY?

Unleash your innermost BEAUTY
Embrace the world...
Your inner beauty
Will always define...
That which is called
Your TOTAL BEAUTY.

Yes, she is pretty
Yes, she is beautiful
But does she possess
What defines...
A good person?
Does she celebrate
When others succeed?

Could that still be...
The person we would call pretty?
The one, we would call beautiful?
Does she still have...
What we would define as
TOTAL BEAUTY?

Therefore, unleash your
Inner-most BEAUTY
Glow in the light of...
What you will call
Your TOTAL BEAUTY.

30

DON'T JUST

Live...
Don't just exist.

Breathe...
Don't just inhale.

Laugh...
Don't just smile.

Dance...
Don't just move.

Cry...
Don't just sob.

Love...
Don't just like.

There's no dress rehearsal
So don't just!

33

34

PART 2

THAT
FEELING

35

LOVE IS IN
THE AIR

Love could be...

Lovely
Oscillating
Vibrant
Exhilarating.

Love might be...

Intentional
Sensual.

Love should be...
Invigorating
Nonchalant.

Love can be...
Tantalising
Humorous
Exciting.

Love will be...
Amorous
Illuminating
Romantic.

LOVE

IS

IN

THE

AIR.

40

MAKE THAT CALL

You call
I call.

What if
I don't call?

What if
You don't call?

41

Who should call?

Someone, please
JUST MAKE THAT CALL.

He calls
She calls

What if
He doesn't call?

What if
She doesn't call?

Who should call?

Someone, please
JUST MAKE THAT CALL

Love will dissipate
If you do not
Communicate.

Go ahead...
Someone, please
JUST MAKE THAT CALL

43

How else can you relate
When distance keeps you
From being intimate

Go ahead...
Someone, please
JUST MAKE THAT CALL

Love will surely
Fade away, if
you both fail to...
SIMPLY
MAKE THAT CALL.

45

46

YOU STILL LOVE ME

Day and night
Summer and winter.

Autumn and Spring
Sunshine and rain.

Yet through it all
You still love me.

47

Laughter or tears
Hope and despair.

Success or failure
Love and heartbreak.

Yet through it all
You still love me.

Fast and slow
Running or walking.

48

High and low
Sitting or standing.

Yet through it all
You still love me. . .
Endlessly!

50

WINDOWS
OF MY HEART

WHEN you look through
The windows of my heart
What do you see?

When I look out of
The windows of my heart
What do I see?

You see...
It is dark?
I see the blinds drawn
I see the curtains closed.

Don't walk away
I will pull up the blinds
I will open the curtains.

WHEN you look through
The windows of my heart
What do you see?

52

When I look out of
The windows of my heart
What do I see?

You see...
It is not clear?
I see it's dusty
I see it's misty.

You don't need your glasses
I will take that cloth
I will wipe it clean.

Whatever you see...
DO LET ME KNOW!

I might see...
Something different
I might see...
Something I can change.

So don't walk away...
From the windows
Of my heart.

54

I'd rather...
You let me know
What it is you see
Through the windows
Of my heart.

56

LOVE

The love I feel for you
Words can't describe.

Sometimes it hurts so bad
I want to cry.

Yet through it all
I know you care.

What can I do now
Without you here?

Love makes me cry
Love makes me smile
Love even keeps me warm
And sometimes...
Love even leaves me cold.

Though time flies by
The sun still comes out
Day after day...
After day.

The moon and stars
Light up the..
Dark, black sky
Each and every night.

How I wish
I could rewind the clock...
Just so I could relive...
Some of those
treasured memories.

Love makes me cry
Love makes me smile
Love even keeps me warm
And sometimes...
Love even leaves me cold.

60

DON'T LOOK BACK

Walk away
Don't look back.

Forget it happened
Look to the future.

Yes, it's unknown
Yes, it seems scary.

The **ONE** above
Will meet your needs.

Shake it off
Dust it clean.

Hold up your head
Throw back those shoulders.

One step, two steps
Three steps...

Strut your stuff...
Just don't look back!

63

64

PART 3

POLY
TICS

66

I AM
A CONTINENT

Africa!
AFRICA?

Africa is but a continent
Not a country
Marvel at its beauty
Celebrate its diversity.

Black and white
Green to Gold
Sandy dunes of the Namib to
Snow caps of Rwenzori.

Where then...
Are your countries, AFRICA?

Eritrea to Madagascar
Lesotho to Djibouti
Number one to
Number fifty-four!

Why then...
Tell me!
Why then...
Do you say AFRICA
As though, I am
But a country?

I am a continent
Africa cries out!

70

MY COLOURS

Green, yellow, red
Yellow, green, red
No! Red, yellow, black.

Those are all wrong
It's red, yellow, green
and a black star
in the middle.

The Black Star
in the middle of...
The bright, vibrant yellow.

Red for the blood of
our forefathers...
Their strife and struggle.

Yellow for the endless
amount of gold...
And other countless
mineral resources.

Green... Oh what greenery...
I have to take my time...
And brag a bit.
The rich vibrant green...
Of the trees.
The bright coloured green...
Of the plants.

And that somewhat...
Lighter green...
Of the grass
which stretches...
For miles...
And miles...
And miles...

ARE YOU DONE?
No. Not quite yet.
Last but not least
The big black star
which from that centre
gleams and sparkles...
And shines.

Oh how it shines!
On the red, the yellow
and also on the green.
It's rays reflect these words...
Freedom
FREEdom
FREEDOM!

FREEDOM to wear
these colours...
With lots of pride.

FREEDOM to hoist myself...
Up high in the sky.

And FREEDOM to...
Just drape down
and be as still...
As the air, would command.

All this while, **JUSTICE**
waltzes gracefully
around the edge.
A constant reminder, that
FREEDOM only exists...
Within the confines
of the perimeter, thus created...
As **JUSTICE** floats around.

Now I'm done...
Let me pause a while
as you also speak...
Of those colours
you are oh... so
proud to wear!

78

DISCOMBOBULATING DILEMMA

Bribery

Corruption

Hold on a minute...

Lobbying

Campaigning.

He gives... before
He gives... after
He gives... during
He still gives!

When is it right?
When is it wrong?

Which is good?
Which is bad?

Or is it just the name...
That makes it
Right or wrong?

Or the name...
Which makes it
Good or bad?

Herein lies...
A seemingly endless
Discombobulating
Dilemma.

82

SPEAK UP

SPEAK UP

Do not offend
Do not insult.

SPEAK UP

But do not start a **war.**

SPEAK UP

Make your point
Do not get emotional.

SPEAK UP

But do not start a **war.**

SPEAK UP

Express your emotions
Don't bottle them in.

84

SPEAK UP

But do not start a **war.**

SPEAK UP

You have an opinion
Give it a voice.

SPEAK UP

But do not start a **war.**

85

Did you just...
Say something?

SPEAK UP

I could barely hear...
For that was...
But a mere _whisper!_

88

DON'T TAKE AWAY
MY FREEDOM

I was born... **f r e e**
I will die... **f r e e.**

Do not take away my...
F r e e d o m
Don't even contemplate
Taking away my...
F r e e d o m.

I live by your rules
But first and foremost
I live by God's rules.

Next time you want to
Curtail my...
F r e e d o m
Ask the ONE above?
'Do I have the freedom
To take away...
Another's...
F r e e d o m?'

90

Maybe not today
Maybe not tomorrow
But maybe, one day
You might just...
Have to answer
For every single time
You took away...
My...
F r e e d o m.

So... **p l e a s e**...
Don't take away...
My...
F r e e d o m.

92

SAY IT AS IT IS

Body Politic...
Party poly-tics.

Two party state
Or four party state?

Three party state
Or five party state?

Multi-party state
Or is that
De-mo-cra-cy?

Democracy!
Freedom of speech
Rule by the people
For the people.

Is it truly
Multi-party?

These are always
The choices.

Labour or
Conservative?

Democrat or
Republican?

It always ends with TWO...
Is it one
Or is it the other?

Alas! Perhaps!
Government...
Is but a replica
Of a family unit?

Mother
Father...
Making the
Decisions.

Do they agree?
Sometimes they do...
But alas...
Not all the time.

Majority...
Minority.

Do they agree?
Should they agree?!

They should still
Nonetheless...
Have but one goal...
To move their
Beloved country...
Forward.

Alas! Perhaps!
Could it be...
That eventually
The human mind...
Will only really process
That choice...
Between the TWO.

The choice of...
Will it be this one
Or will it be the other?

Rethink it...
Redefine it.

Say it as it is!

De-mo-cra-cy...
Eventually
Equates to...
No more than...
A two party state not
A multi party state.

100

PRESS ON.
INCH FORWARD!

We yearned for...
Freedom.

We strived for...
Independence.

Independence and freedom
Are ours...
Now and forever.

101

We thrive in the knowledge
That decisions we make
Are not yours, but rather
Ours to live by.

Decisions to go
Decisions to come.

Decisions to walk
Decisions to run.

Decisions to start
Decisions to stop.

STOP?!

102

Please permit me...
I also have to STOP
And ponder.

Human beings retire
Countries can not.

There's still so much
For you to acquiesce.

SO PRESS ON...
INCH FORWARD...

103

Surely, at some point...
SUCCESS will smile broadly
As she eventually says...
It is my great pleasure
To finally be...
Acquainted with you.

105

106

PART 4

FORGET
THE
'TO DO'

108

SOUL FOOD
RESTAURANT

Welcome to the...
Soul Food Restaurant.

It's nice you chose...
To come and dine
here today.

109

We have on the menu...
A five course meal
served with slow jam.
Not just any jam
but the ultimate...
Luther slow jam.

For our three course meal
you have the choice of...
Some more slow jams.
Will it be Anita Baker
or the sultry Regina Belle?

We also have some salad...
The perfect mix of
Roberta Flack and
Sadao Watanabe...
Jazz meets R & B.

As a starter...
We serve up a soup
with croissants...
None other than
some more Luther...
With the diva
Mariah Carey.

We have some exotic
meals as well...
Jamaican cuisine...
Gregory Isaacs and
the smooth Tyrone Taylor.
In case you thought...
Some rice 'n' peas
was amiss on our menu.

How about some...
Old English cuisine?
I'm talking...
Spandau Ballet
or Phil Collins.

112

Our special gives you
fast food, Nigerian style.
The energetic Mr. Real...
On a shaku shaku level...
Or maybe flame grills...
Courtesy David-O's 'Fia.'

You might be wandering
what dessert would be.
Hmmm... Now that is
some authentic classical tunes...
Courtesy Mozart Or
Johann Sebastian Strauss...

You chose the five course...
Luther slow jam style?
Believe me...
That's 'So Amazing.'

That choice also comes with
Marvin Gaye...
'on the house.'

We hope you enjoy this...
while the chef cooks your
Luther five course meal.

No tips please...
Some suggestions instead
to our worldwide menu...
Will do just fine. Thank you.

We hope you choose us...
The Soul Food Restaurant
the next time you hunger...
for some more
scrumptious, delicious
heart warming, Soul Food.

116

ON THAT
WARM BRIDGE

I decide to meet
And have some tea...

I'm here already
Where could you be?

You will be late?
Oh! Don't you worry...

117

Waiter, please bring
Your finest tea.

No need for sugar
Just frothy, white cream.

He saunters back
With steaming, hot tea.

I add the cream
I stir the mix.

And this is when
My science kicks in.

I always judge
the warmth of my tea...
Since there's a tiny bridge
across which...
I can savour
that sweet taste of tea.

I raise the cup up close
I see the steam rise up
I inhale the aroma...
Which could only come...
From an enticing...
Cup of tea.

I take a sip...
Ouch! That sure did...
Give me a burn...
I grab some water
to cool that down.

I wait a few more minutes
as I muse, at the...
Chitter-chatter...
That fills the room.

I lift my cup...
To try again.

This time, I take a sip...
But slower than before...
Oh boy! It feels just right
No scalded tongue...
This time around.

Just calming and relaxing...
As I take a deep breath...
And sink much further
in my chair.

I finally found that bridge...
That warm and silky bridge...
Which spans...
From hot to cold.

The minute it is cold...
I want the tea no more...
And when it Is served hot...
Those burns...
I must avoid.

And after all these years...
Of sipping on my tea...
I still have not
achieved success...
On that hot
and cold divide.

Oh! No...
The tea is now too cold
Waiter...
Please...
Some more hot tea...

Oh! There you are...

Kiss, kiss...

Hug, hug...

Sit, sit.

Next time, I'll try
to get it right...
To sip and finish all my tea...
On that warm bridge
which always spans...
That seemingly narrow gap...
Between, it's too hot
and now it's too cold.

125

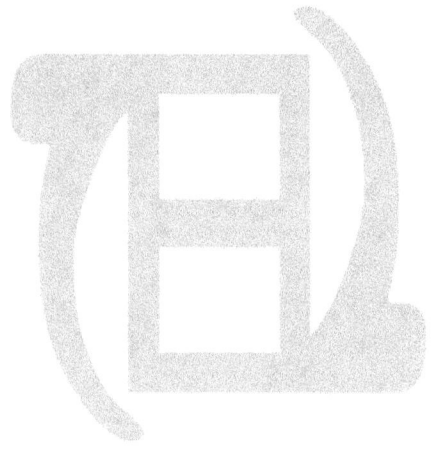

126

TANGO AMONGST
THE CLOUDS

Fasten your seatbelts...
This is your captain speaking
We will be cruising at...

The plane starts to move...
Slowly at first
Then it picks up speed.

127

Everything flies past...
As I gaze out of
the plane's tiny window.

My tummy heaves downwards
as if it would escape...
Straight out of the frame
of my tense, cringing body.

I feel those pins and needles...
Somewhere deep in my ears
I'm thrown backwards, rudely
as I sink further in my seat.

My nose now points upwards
as though to replicate...
The ginormous, rounded nose
of this aerodynamic plane.

The babies start crying...
The mothers calm them down.

My ears now start aching
Oh no!
Not that terrible earache
beginning once again.

I grab a sweet
Oh dear! My earplugs...
Ah! There they are
Right by my side
Where they have been...
All of this time.

Now this is when, I can relax...
This is when, I can stay calm.

It is now the time...
For the food, the drinks...
The in-flight, captivating
entertainment.

I have my phone...
Yet I have no calls.

This is surely the one time
when I can truly say...
I have firmly shut the door...
On all the noise...
That emanates...
From this our ever
changing world.

It is heavenly bliss...
I'm in the midst of the clouds...
No, I'm above the clouds...
Now, I'm beneath the clouds.

Oh what calm!
Oh what serenity!
Oh what tranquillity!

How I wish ...
I could reach out and touch...
Those clouds, which appear
to beckon me close.

It simply feels like heaven
At least I think...
This is how it would feel...
To be in heaven.

132

Fly
Fly
Fly Me Away...

Oh dear!
What's this...
My thoughts are
sharply curtailed...
This is your captain speaking...
We are about to begin
our descent...

133

Is it over?
How can we be heading...
to land so soon?
We are actually returning...
to the noise of our world.

Oh well!
We have no choice...
I can only look forward to
my next tango...
Amongst the clouds.

134

135

136

PART 5

MATHE-
MATI-
CALLY
POETIC

137

138

ONE PLUS ONE

One plus one
Is always two.

If it's right
It's right.

If it's wrong
It's wrong.

Get it right
And get your marks.

That's the joy
Of doing maths.

141

142

GEO-ME-TREE

Square and cube
Circle and sphere.

Which is two-D?
Which is three-D?

Triangle is two-D
Prism is three-D.

Trian-gular Prism...
What could that be?

Is it two-D?
Is it three-D?

Three dimensional...
That's what it is.

Learn it once...
You won't forget.

And guess what?
That's geo-me-tree
For you!

144

145

146

PIE NOT PI (π)

Calcul-us
Radi-us...
Are you talking
about us?

Geometry
Trigono-metry...
I know that
There is symmetry.

147

Multiplication
Division...
Now you bring me
much more of this tension.

Decagon
Heptagon...
Is there possibly
another dragon?

Diameter
Perimeter...
I know I could do with
some more of twitter.

148

Dodecahedron
Icosahedron…
Are they all parts, of that
big, black new cauldron?

Kilogram
Milligram…
You mean they are
available on Instagram?

Pie chart
Pythagoras…
I'd rather, more PI
less maths

What I meant to say
was pie, and guess what...
I realize... I said PI.
Please, no more maths...
Thank you!

150

152

OVER ONE

Jump
Somersault
Land on ONE.

ONE is... Shaking
ONE is... Swaying.

Jump off ONE or...
You might just fall.

153

You can stand alone
You will stand alone
You don't need ONE
To help you stand.

As a fraction or
In division
You'll always find...
That in the end...
Any number standing
Over ONE...
Will also stand and shine
All by itself.

155

156

PART 6

MYSTIC

158

PLEASE DON'T STAND STILL

I sit still...
I feel...
The air.

I start moving...
I feel...
More air.

159

The air feels warm.
THEN JUST STAND STILL.

The air feels cold.
I should still stand still?

Guess what!
I did stand still...
For just one moment...
But the wind did not...
It just refused

It blew
To the left.

                It blew
                  To the right.

WIND, PLEASE...
Can you stand still?
I really don't want...
To feel such cold air...
SWIRLING
All around me.

161

I cannot see the air...
Yet, I cannot live...
Without the air.

Does it really matter
That I do not see...
The air?

This is what
I can say that I see
The branches swaying
The leaves flapping
The rain drops moving...

162

Right

Centre

Left

And   sometimes

Centre

Left

Right...

163

And what a sight it is...
When all I can do...
Is stop for just a moment...
And gaze at those
Fluffy, white snow flakes...
As they flutter haphazardly
Down, from the sky above.

Okay... this time, WIND...
Please don't stand still
I need you to move...
So I can see...
That invaluable air
Which I so desperately...
Need to live.

164

165

166

MAGIC

It's there...
I blink
It's not there...
Again, I blink.

I saw it there...
I blinked
I didn't see it there...
I blinked, again.

This is definitely...
A show of utter Magic!

It's liquid...
I look
It's solid...
Again, I look.

It's liquid again...
I look
Now, it's solid...
I'm still looking.

This is purely...
A magical display!

Whether I look
Or whether I blink
It still seems...
There's an unbelievable...
Show of magic!

170

THANK YOU

I thought
About it

I wrote
It all down

You read
Through it all

171

I truly hope...
There's one poem
You 'kinda' like.

Permit me
To also say...
THANK YOU
Lots and lots...
For all your time.

Now this is where
I draw the curtain...
With these
Three letter words...

THE

N

D.

174

APPENDIX:

ADINKRA SYMBOLS

The Adinkra symbols of Ghana are used, mainly in this book, for their designs, as opposed to their meanings.

Each Adinkra symbol represents a unique Ghanaian 'proverb' which in turn depicts part of the Ghanaian culture. The names of the symbols shown are provided on subsequent pages. These names are in Twi, which is the language of the Akan people in Ghana.

PAGE	ADINKRA SYMBOL
0	GYE NYAME 'EXCEPT FOR GOD'
2	NYINKYIM 'TWISTING'
4	ABUSUA PA 'GOOD FAMILY'
8	NKONTIMSEFO MPUA 'HAIR OF THE QUEEN'S SERVANT'
14	OSRAM NE NSORAMMA 'THE MOON AND THE STAR'
20	BOA ME NA ME MMOA WU 'HELP ME AND LET ME HELP YOU'
26	DUAFE 'WOODEN COMB'
30	FAWOHODIE 'INDEPENDENCE'
34	NYAME DUA 'GOD'S TREE/ALTAR'

176

PAGE	ADINKRA SYMBOL
36	NEA OPE SE NKROFOO YE MAWO NO, YE SAA ARA MA WON 'WHAT YOU WANT PEOPLE TO DO FOR YOU, DO THE SAME FOR THEM'
41	ASASE YE DURU 'THE EARTH IS HEAVY'
47	NYANSAPO 'WISDOM KNOT'
50	ABAN 'FENCE'
56	NYA GYIDIE 'HAVE FAITH'
60	ONYANKOPON ANIWA 'GOD'S EYE'
64	ESONO ANANTAM 'ELEPHANT'S FOOTPRINT
66	MAKO NYINAA MPATU MMERE 'ALL PEPPERS DO NOT RIPEN AT THE SAME TIME'

PAGE	ADINKRA SYMBOL
70	OKUAFO PA 'GOOD FARMER'
78	MPATAPO 'KNOT OF PACIFICATION'
82	TUMI TESE KOSUA 'POWER IS LIKE AN EGG'
88	SOM ONYANKOPON 'WORSHIP GOD'
92	NTEASEE 'UNDERSTANDING'
100	MATE MASIE 'I HAVE KEPT WHAT I HAVE HEARD'
106	DWENNI MMEN 'RAM'S HORNS
108	SANKOFA 'RETUN AND TAKE IT'
116	GYAWU ATIKO 'THE BACK OF GYAWU'S HEAD'

178

PAGE	ADINKRA SYMBOL
126	ONYANKOPON NE YEN NTENA 'GOD SHOULD LIVE WITH US'
136	UAC NKANEA 'UAC LIGHTS'
138	TABONO 'PADDLE/ OAR'
142	NEA OPE SE OBEDI HENE 'HE WHO WANTS TO BE KING'
146	NEA ONNIM NO, SUA A OHU 'HE WHO DOES NOT KNOW, CAN KNOW FROM LEARNING'
152	TAMFO BEBRE 'THE ENEMY WILL SUFFER'
156	ABODE SANTANN 'ALL SEEING EYE'
158	OWIA KOKROKO 'GREATNESS OF THE SUN'

179

PAGE	ADINKRA SYMBOL
166	ANANSE NTONTAN 'SPIDER'S WEB'
170	KAE ME 'REMEMBER ME'
174	WOFORO DUA PA A 'WHEN YOU CLIMB A GREAT TREE'
175	SESA WO SUBAN 'CHANGE OR TRANSFORM YOUR CHARACTER'

www.ingramcontent.com/pod-product-compliance
Lightning Source LLC
Chambersburg PA
CBHW051511170626
46811CB00002B/759